CSID EL

DIET COOKBOOK

Step-By-Step Meal Plan Guide, Delicious Recipes, And Essential Food Lists Tailored For Beginners To Navigate Sucrose Intolerance With Ease And Confidence"

Amos jimmy

TABLE OF CONTENT

INTRODUCTION

Welcome to the "CSID Elimination Diet Cookbook," a pioneering guide designed to transform the way individuals with Congenital Sucrase-Isomaltase Deficiency (CSID) approach their dietary needs. CSID, a condition where the body lacks the enzymes necessary to digest certain sugars and carbohydrates, can lead to a range of digestive discomforts and challenges. This cookbook is born out of a deep understanding of these challenges and a passionate commitment to offering solutions that are not only effective but also enjoyable and sustainable.

Our journey into the realm of dietary management for CSID began with a simple premise: everyone deserves to enjoy food, regardless of their dietary restrictions. It was this belief that propelled us to seek out, develop, and refine recipes that would not only adhere to the strict dietary requirements of those with CSID but also delight the taste buds and nourish the body. What we have created is more than just a cookbook; it's a tool for empowerment, a source of inspiration, and a guide to rediscovering the joy of eating.

Within these pages, you will find a carefully curated collection of recipes that eliminate the specific carbohydrates and sugars that individuals with CSID cannot properly digest. From hearty breakfasts to satisfying main courses, from snacks to desserts, each recipe has been designed with both health and flavor in mind. Our goal is to provide a diverse range of dishes that will cater to all tastes and occasions, ensuring that adhering to a CSID-friendly diet does not mean sacrificing variety or pleasure in your meals.

Moreover, this cookbook serves as an educational resource, offering insights into CSID, the science behind the diet, and practical tips for navigating food choices in everyday life. Whether you are newly diagnosed with CSID, a caregiver to someone with the condition, or a seasoned veteran in managing dietary restrictions, this book aims to support and enhance your dietary journey.

CHAPTER 1

UNDERSTANDING CSID

The CSID (Congenital Sucrase-Isomaltase Deficiency) elimination diet is a specialized nutritional approach designed for individuals with CSID, a condition that affects the way one's body digests certain sugars. Before diving into the benefits and how it works, let's take a moment to understand the condition and the history of this dietary intervention.

CSID is a rare genetic disorder that impairs the ability of the intestine to break down and absorb two specific types of sugar: sucrose (table sugar) and maltose (a sugar found in grains). This is due to the deficiency of two enzymes, sucrase and isomaltase, which are essential for the digestion of these sugars. When individuals with CSID consume foods containing sucrose or maltose, they often experience symptoms like bloating, gas, diarrhea, and abdominal pain.

The History of the CSID Elimination Diet

The CSID elimination diet emerged as a response to the need for managing the uncomfortable and sometimes debilitating symptoms associated with the condition. Prior to understanding the genetic basis of CSID, patients often went undiagnosed or misdiagnosed, leading to ineffective treatments. With advancements in genetic testing and a deeper understanding of digestive biochemistry, the late 20th and early 21st centuries saw a more targeted approach to managing CSID, including dietary interventions.

This elimination diet focuses on removing foods that contain sucrose and maltose, thereby reducing the burden on the digestive system of individuals with CSID. It's a strategy that has evolved over years, informed by clinical research and the practical experiences of dietitians working with CSID patients.

5 Benefits of the CSID Elimination Diet

- **Reduced Digestive Symptoms:** The most immediate and impactful benefit is the significant reduction in digestive distress. By eliminating the sugars that individuals with CSID cannot properly digest, symptoms such as bloating, gas, and diarrhea can be greatly minimized or even eliminated.

- **Improved Nutrient Absorption:** With the reduction of undigested sugars in the intestine, the body can better absorb other nutrients from food, which are crucial for overall health. This can lead to improved energy levels, better immune function, and a reduction in deficiencies that might have been exacerbated by malabsorption.

- **Enhanced Quality of Life:** Living with chronic digestive symptoms can be challenging and affect one's quality of life. The CSID elimination diet can offer a path towards a more comfortable and fulfilling daily experience, allowing individuals to engage in activities without the constant worry of their symptoms.

- **Personalized Nutrition:** The process of implementing the CSID elimination diet often involves working closely with a dietitian to identify which foods trigger symptoms. This personalized approach not only helps manage CSID but also educates individuals about their bodies and how different foods affect them, fostering a more mindful relationship with eating.
- **Prevention of Long-Term Complications**: By consistently adhering to the diet, individuals can prevent the chronic effects of malabsorption and malnutrition, such as weakened bones or impaired growth in children. This proactive approach can help mitigate future health issues.

Implementing the CSID Elimination Diet

Starting the CSID elimination diet can be daunting, but it's about taking one step at a time. Initially, it involves identifying and eliminating foods high in sucrose and maltose. This might mean saying goodbye to certain sweets, processed foods, and some grains, but it also opens up a world of foods that are safe and nourishing.

Grocery List

Proteins:
- Chicken Breast - Lean protein source, versatile for cooking.
- Salmon Fillets - Rich in omega-3 fatty acids, good for heart and brain health.
- Ground Turkey - Low in fat, high in protein, suitable for making meatballs or patties.
- Eggs - Complete protein source, rich in vitamins D and B12.

Dairy or Dairy Alternatives:
- Lactose-Free Greek Yogurt - High in protein and calcium, without the lactose that can trigger symptoms.
- Lactose-Free Cheese or Nutritional Yeast - For calcium intake and flavor enhancement in meals.

Grains:
- Quinoa - A complete protein and fiber source, gluten-free.
- Gluten-Free Pasta - For creating CSID-friendly pasta dishes.
- Rice Cakes - Low in fermentable carbohydrates, suitable for snacking.

- Fruits (Low in Sucrose and Maltose):
- Avocado - Provides healthy fats and fiber.
- Blueberries and Strawberries - Low in fructose, high in antioxidants and vitamins.
- Kiwi and Papaya - Rich in vitamins and digestive enzymes, aiding in protein digestion.

Vegetables:
- Zucchini and Cucumbers - High in water content and vitamins, low in fermentable carbohydrates.
- Bell Peppers - Rich in vitamin C and antioxidants, add color and flavor to dishes.
- Leafy Greens (Spinach, Kale, Lettuce) - High in iron and vitamins A, C, and K.
- Broccoli and Cauliflower - High in fiber and vitamins, to be consumed in moderation based on tolerance.

Healthy Fats:
- Olive Oil - For cooking and dressings, rich in monounsaturated fats.
- Coconut Oil - A medium-chain triglyceride, easier to digest for some.

Sweeteners (CSID Friendly):
- Stevia - A natural sweetener that does not contribute to CSID symptoms.

- Erythritol - A sugar alcohol that is generally well-tolerated.

Miscellaneous:
- Herbs and Spices (e.g., Dill, Cilantro, Mint) - For flavoring dishes without adding sugars.
- Lemon and Lime - For adding flavor to water or dishes, rich in vitamin C.
- Almond Milk or Coconut Milk - Lactose-free alternatives for cooking and baking.

Snacks:
- Rice Cakes - A light and versatile snack.
- Homemade Vegetable Chips - Made from kale, zucchini, or sweet potatoes, baked with a touch of olive oil.

CHAPTER 2

BREAKFAST RECIPES

Berry Avocado Smoothie Bowl

Serves: 1

Cooking Time: 10 minutes

Ingredients:

- Avocado (High in healthy fats, fiber, CSID friendly): 1/2 medium
- Blueberries (Rich in antioxidants, vitamins, CSID friendly): 1/4 cup
- Blackberries (High in vitamins C and K, fiber, CSID friendly): 1/4 cup
- Coconut milk (Lactose-free, rich in vitamins C, E, B1, B3, B5, and B6, CSID friendly): 1/2 cup
- Chia seeds (High in omega-3 fatty acids, fiber, CSID friendly): 1 tablespoon
- Honey (Natural sweetener, tolerated by some CSID patients): 1 teaspoon **Substitution:** Maple syrup (Low sucrose, CSID friendly): 1 teaspoon

Instructions:

- **Prepare the Ingredients:** Start by preparing all your ingredients. Cut the avocado in half, remove the pit, and scoop out 1/2 of the avocado flesh. Measure the blueberries, blackberries, coconut milk, chia seeds, and your choice of sweetener.
- **Blend the Smoothie Base:** Combine the avocado, blueberries, blackberries, coconut milk, chia seeds, and honey or maple syrup in a blender. Blend until the mixture is smooth. If the smoothie seems too thick, adjust the consistency by adding a bit more coconut milk until it reaches your preferred thickness.
- **Serve:** Transfer the smoothie into a bowl. For an extra touch, garnish with some additional berries and a sprinkle of chia seeds.

Scientific Notes:

- Avocado is rich in monounsaturated fats, essential for brain development and nutrient absorption, making it ideal for those with CSID without exacerbating symptoms.
- Blueberries and blackberries are packed with essential vitamins and antioxidants, promoting immune health.

Their low sucrose content makes them suitable for CSID diets.

- Coconut milk serves as an excellent dairy alternative for CSID patients, offering necessary vitamins without the lactose.
- Chia seeds provide omega-3 fatty acids, important for brain health. Their high fiber content is generally well-tolerated by CSID patients in small amounts.

Nutritional Information:

- Calories: 350 kcal
- Protein: 4 g
- Fat: 24 g
- Saturated Fat: 7 g
- Monounsaturated Fat: 10 g
- Carbohydrates: 34 g
- Dietary Fiber: 14 g

Kiwi & Papaya Fruit Salad

Serves: 1

Cooking Time: 10 minutes

Ingredients:

- Kiwifruit (Rich in vitamins C and K, fiber, CSID friendly): 1 medium, diced
- Papaya (High in vitamin C, folate, and digestive enzymes, CSID friendly): 1/2 cup, diced
- Fresh mint leaves (Adds flavor, aids digestion, CSID friendly): 1 tablespoon, chopped
- Lime juice (High in vitamin C, enhances flavor, CSID friendly): 1 tablespoon
- Coconut flakes (Adds texture, nutrients, CSID friendly): 1 tablespoon

Instructions:

- **Prepare the Ingredients**: Dice the kiwifruit and papaya into small pieces. Chop the fresh mint leaves finely.
- **Mix the Salad:** In a bowl, combine the diced kiwifruit and papaya. Add the chopped mint leaves and toss gently.

- **Dress the Salad:** Drizzle the lime juice over the salad and sprinkle with coconut flakes. Mix gently to combine.

Scientific Notes:

- Kiwifruit and papaya are excellent sources of vitamins C and K. Papaya contains papain, an enzyme that aids digestion, making these fruits suitable for CSID.
- Fresh mint is known for its digestive benefits and adds refreshing flavor without adding sugars problematic for CSID.
- Lime juice adds a zest of flavor and vitamin C without the sugars found in other citrus fruits, aligning with CSID dietary considerations.
- Coconut flakes provide a crunchy texture and are a good source of healthy fats and fiber in moderation for CSID patients.

Nutritional Information (Estimated):

- Calories: 150 kcal
- Protein: 2 g
- Fat: 5 g
- Saturated Fat: 4 g
- Carbohydrates: 27 g

- Dietary Fiber: 5 g

Oatmeal with Pear & Cinnamon

Serves: 1

Cooking Time: 15 minutes

Ingredients:

- Gluten-free oats (High in fiber, iron, and protein, CSID friendly): 1/2 cup
- Pear (Rich in fiber, vitamins C and K, CSID friendly): 1/2 medium, diced
- Cinnamon (Controls blood sugar levels, adds flavor, CSID friendly): 1/4 teaspoon
- Almond milk (Lactose-free, rich in calcium and vitamin E, CSID friendly): 1 cup
- Walnuts (High in omega-3 fatty acids, protein, tolerated by few CSID patients): 1 tablespoon, chopped
- Substitution: Pumpkin seeds (Rich in magnesium, omega-3, CSID friendly): 1 tablespoon

Instructions:

- **Cook the Oatmeal:** In a small saucepan, bring the almond milk to a boil. Add the gluten-free oats and reduce the heat to simmer. Cook for about 5-7 minutes, stirring occasionally, until the oats are soft and have absorbed most of the liquid.

- **Add Flavors and Toppings:** Stir the diced pear and cinnamon into the oatmeal. Cook for an additional 2-3 minutes.
- **Serve with Toppings:** Pour the oatmeal into a bowl. Top with chopped walnuts or pumpkin seeds for added texture and nutrients.

Scientific Notes:

- Gluten-free oats are a solid source of fiber and nutrients, suitable for CSID patients by avoiding gluten.
- Pears provide fiber and essential nutrients, aiding digestion and suitable for CSID.
- Cinnamon helps control blood sugar levels and adds flavor without sugar, fitting the CSID diet.
- Almond milk offers a lactose-free alternative rich in calcium and vitamin E.
- Walnuts, while nutritious, may be problematic for some CSID patients; pumpkin seeds are a suitable substitute, offering magnesium and omega-3 fatty acids.

Nutritional Information (Estimated):

- Calories: 300 kcal
- Protein: 8 g
- Fat: 15 g
- Saturated Fat: 1.5 g
- Carbohydrates: 37 g
- Dietary Fiber: 7 g

Cherry Almond Oatmeal

Serves: 1

Cooking Time: 15 minutes

Ingredients:

- Gluten-free oats (High in fiber, CSID friendly): 1/2 cup
- Fresh cherries (Rich in antioxidants, vitamin C, CSID friendly): 1/4 cup, pitted and chopped
- Almond milk (Lactose-free, rich in vitamin E, CSID friendly): 3/4 cup
- Almonds (Rich in healthy fats, vitamin E, tolerated by few CSID patients): 1 tablespoon, slivered
- Substitution: Sunflower seeds (Rich in vitamin E, magnesium, CSID friendly): 1 tablespoon
- Ground flaxseed (High in omega-3 fatty acids, fiber, CSID friendly): 1 teaspoon
- Cinnamon (Anti-inflammatory properties, CSID friendly): 1/4 teaspoon

Instructions:

- **Cook the Oatmeal**: In a saucepan, bring the almond milk to a boil. Add the gluten-free oats and reduce the heat to simmer. Cook for about 5-7 minutes, stirring occasionally, until the oats are soft and most of the milk has been absorbed.

- **Add the Cherries:** Stir in the chopped cherries and continue to cook for an additional 2-3 minutes, allowing the cherries to warm through and release their juices.
- **Serve with Toppings**: Transfer the cooked oatmeal into a bowl. Top with slivered almonds or sunflower seeds, sprinkle with ground flaxseed, and cinnamon for flavor.

Scientific Notes:

- Gluten-free oats provide soluble fiber, aiding digestion without overwhelming the CSID digestive system.
- Cherries offer antioxidants, supporting immune health and reducing inflammation, suitable for CSID.
- Almond milk is a dairy-free alternative rich in vitamins, supporting growth and bone health.
- Almonds and sunflower seeds supply essential fatty acids and vitamin E, crucial for skin health and immune function. Almonds may be substituted with sunflower seeds for those sensitive.

- Ground flaxseed contributes omega-3 fatty acids, beneficial for brain development, and fiber for healthy digestion.

Nutritional Information (Estimated):

- Calories: 280 kcal
- Protein: 8 g
- Fat: 15 g
- Saturated Fat: 1 g
- Carbohydrates: 33 g
- Dietary Fiber: 7 g

Papaya Lime Yogurt Parfait

Serves: 1

Cooking Time: 5 minutes

Ingredients:

- Greek yogurt, lactose-free (High in protein, calcium, CSID friendly): 1/2 cup
- Papaya (Rich in digestive enzymes, vitamins C and A, CSID friendly): 1/2 cup, diced
- Lime zest (Adds flavor, vitamin C, CSID friendly): 1 teaspoon
- Coconut flakes (Adds texture, nutrients, CSID friendly): 1 tablespoon
- Honey (Natural sweetener, tolerated by some CSID patients): 1 teaspoon
- Substitution: Stevia (Natural sweetener, CSID friendly): 1/4 teaspoon

Instructions:

- **Layer the Parfait:** In a glass or bowl, start by layering half of the lactose-free Greek yogurt at the bottom.

- **Add Fruits and Flavors:** Add a layer of diced papaya on top of the yogurt. Sprinkle half of the lime zest and coconut flakes.
- **Repeat Layers and Sweeten:** Add the remaining yogurt, then top with the rest of the papaya, lime zest, and coconut flakes. Sweeten with honey or stevia according to preference.

Scientific Notes:

- Lactose-free Greek yogurt offers high protein and calcium, essential for growth and bone health, without lactose that triggers CSID symptoms.
- Papaya contains papain, aiding protein digestion, and is rich in vitamins for CSID diets.
- Lime zest enhances flavor and provides vitamin C, supporting the immune system without added sugar.
- Coconut flakes add texture and healthy fats, beneficial in moderation.
- Honey might not be suitable for all CSID patients; stevia is a safe alternative sweetener.

Nutritional Information (Estimated):

- Calories: 200 kcal
- Protein: 10 g

- Fat: 6 g
- Saturated Fat: 4 g
- Carbohydrates: 28 g
- Dietary Fiber: 3 g

Avocado & Egg Breakfast Wrap

Serves: 1

Cooking Time: 10 minutes

Ingredients:

- Gluten-free tortillas (CSID friendly): 1 large
- Eggs (High in protein, vitamins D and B12, CSID friendly): 2, scrambled
- Avocado (Rich in healthy fats, fiber, CSID friendly): 1/4, sliced
- Spinach (Rich in iron, vitamins, CSID friendly): 1/4 cup, raw
- Olive oil (For cooking, healthy fat, CSID friendly): 1 teaspoon
- Salt (CSID friendly): to taste
- Pepper (CSID friendly): to taste

Instructions:

- **Prepare the Eggs:** In a skillet, heat the olive oil over medium heat. Scramble the eggs and season with salt and pepper to taste. Cook until the eggs are set but still moist.
- **Warm the Tortilla**: Heat the gluten-free tortilla in a separate pan or in the microwave for a few seconds until warm and flexible.
- **Assemble the Wrap:** Lay the warmed tortilla on a plate. Spread the scrambled eggs across the center of the tortilla. Add the sliced avocado and raw spinach on top of the eggs.
- **Wrap and Serve:** Fold the tortilla over the filling, tucking in the ends, to form a wrap. Serve warm.

Scientific Notes:

- Gluten-free tortillas provide a safe carbohydrate source for CSID, avoiding gluten that can trigger symptoms.
- Eggs offer complete protein and essential vitamins, supporting growth and repair for CSID diets.
- Avocado supplies monounsaturated fats and fiber, aiding cardiovascular health and digestion.

- Spinach contributes vitamins and minerals, including iron and vitamin K, without exacerbating CSID symptoms.
- Olive oil is used for its healthy fats, enhancing absorption of fat-soluble vitamins.

Nutritional Information (Estimated):

- Calories: 400 kcal
- Protein: 14 g
- Fat: 30 g
- Saturated Fat: 6 g
- Carbohydrates: 20 g
- Dietary Fiber: 5 g

Blueberry Quinoa Breakfast Bowl

Serves: 1

Cooking Time: 20 minutes

Ingredients:

- Quinoa (High in protein and fiber, CSID friendly): 1/2 cup cooked
- Blueberries (Rich in antioxidants and vitamins, CSID friendly): 1/4 cup
- Coconut milk (Lactose-free and rich in vitamins, CSID friendly): 1/2 cup
- Sliced almonds (Rich in healthy fats and vitamin E, tolerated by few CSID patients): 1 tablespoon
- Substitution: Hemp seeds (Rich in omega-3 and protein, CSID friendly): 1 tablespoon
- Honey (Natural sweetener, tolerated by some CSID patients): 1 teaspoon
- Substitution: Stevia (Natural sweetener, CSID friendly): 1/4 teaspoon

Instructions:

- **Prepare the Quinoa:** If not already cooked, rinse 1/4 cup uncooked quinoa under cold water, then bring to a boil in 1/2 cup of water. Reduce to a simmer, cover, and cook until all the water is absorbed (about 15 minutes).

- **Warm the Quinoa and Coconut Milk**: In a bowl, combine the cooked quinoa with coconut milk. Warm this mixture, if desired, in a microwave or on the stove until it reaches a comfortable eating temperature.
- **Assemble the Bowl:** To the warm quinoa and coconut milk mixture, add the blueberries. Top with sliced almonds or hemp seeds. Sweeten with honey or stevia according to preference.

Scientific Notes:

- Quinoa provides all nine essential amino acids, making it a complete protein source. Its fiber content supports healthy digestion.
- Blueberries offer a high nutrient profile, essential for immune health without exacerbating CSID symptoms.
- Coconut milk serves as a creamy, lactose-free alternative, enriching the dish with additional vitamins.
- Almonds and hemp seeds supply essential fatty acids and protein. Hemp seeds are a more universally tolerated source for CSID patients.

- Honey may be tolerated by some CSID patients in moderation, but stevia is a safer, calorie-free sweetener for those sensitive to honey.

Nutritional Information (Estimated):

- Calories: 350 kcal
- Protein: 10 g
- Fat: 15 g
- Saturated Fat: 5 g
- Carbohydrates: 45 g
- Dietary Fiber: 8 g

Cranberry and Pear Compote over Gluten-Free Pancakes

Serves: 2

Cooking Time: 30 minutes

Ingredients:

- Gluten-free pancake mix (CSID friendly): 1 cup
- Fresh cranberries (Low in sugar, high in antioxidants, CSID friendly): 1/2 cup
- Pear (Rich in fiber and vitamins, CSID friendly): 1 medium, diced
- Water (For compote, CSID friendly): 1/2 cup
- Maple syrup (Natural sweetener, lower in sucrose, tolerated by some CSID patients): 2 tablespoons
- Substitution: Monk fruit sweetener (Natural sweetener, CSID friendly): 2 tablespoons

Instructions:

- **Prepare the Pancakes:** Mix the gluten-free pancake mix according to package instructions. Cook the pancakes on a hot, lightly oiled griddle or skillet until golden brown on both sides. Keep warm.

- **Make the Compote:** In a saucepan, combine the cranberries, diced pear, and water. Cook over medium heat until the cranberries burst and the pear is tender, about 10 minutes. Sweeten with maple syrup or monk fruit sweetener to taste.
- **Serve:** Place pancakes on plates and top with the warm cranberry and pear compote.

Scientific Notes:

- Gluten-free pancakes provide a safe carbohydrate source for CSID patients, avoiding gluten.
- Cranberries offer antioxidant properties, beneficial for urinary tract health and reducing inflammation.
- Pears are a gentle source of fiber and vitamins, aiding digestion without overwhelming the digestive system.
- Maple syrup contains sucrose and should be used sparingly; monk fruit sweetener is a no-calorie alternative suitable for CSID patients.

Nutritional Information (Estimated for 2 servings):

- Calories: 400 kcal per serving
- Protein: 6 g
- Fat: 10 g
- Saturated Fat: 2 g

- Carbohydrates: 72 g
- Dietary Fiber: 5 g

Lemon and Olive Oil Dressing over Avocado Toast

Serves: 1

Cooking Time: 5 minutes

Ingredients:

- Gluten-free bread (High in fiber, CSID friendly): 1 slice
- Avocado (Rich in healthy fats and fiber, CSID friendly): 1/2, mashed
- Olive oil (Rich in monounsaturated fats, CSID friendly): 1 teaspoon
- Lemon juice (High in vitamin C, aids digestion, CSID friendly): 1 teaspoon
- Fresh basil (Adds flavor, CSID friendly): 1 tablespoon, chopped
- Salt (CSID friendly): to taste
- Pepper (CSID friendly): to taste

Instructions:

- **Toast the Bread:** Toast the slice of gluten-free bread until it is golden and crispy.
- **Prepare the Avocado Mixture:** In a bowl, mash the avocado. Mix in the olive oil, lemon juice, chopped basil, salt, and pepper to taste.
- **Assemble the Toast:** Spread the avocado mixture evenly over the toasted gluten-free bread.
- **Serve:** Enjoy the avocado toast immediately, garnished with additional basil if desired.

Scientific Notes:

- Gluten-free bread allows for the enjoyment of toast without gluten-induced digestive issues.
- Avocado provides essential fats and fibers, promoting heart health and digestion without triggering CSID symptoms.
- Olive oil and lemon juice add flavor and healthy fats, enhancing nutrient absorption and supporting immune function.
- Fresh basil offers flavor without high-sucrose content, suitable for CSID diets.

Nutritional Information (Estimated):

- Calories: 250 kcal
- Protein: 4 g
- Fat: 20 g
- Saturated Fat: 3 g
- Carbohydrates: 18 g
- Dietary Fiber: 7 g

CONGRATULATIONS
ON FINISHING CHAPTER 2

Congratulations on finishing Chapter 2 of our csid diet guide! I hope you've enjoyed exploring our breakfast recipes and have found them to be not only delicious but also supportive of your csid management goals.

It's important to remember that each recipe in this guide has been carefully crafted to exclude ingredients that are known to trigger csid symptoms, so you can cook and enjoy your meals without worrying about problem. By following these recipes, you're taking a positive step towards improving your overall well-being.

Now, let's dive into the world of lunch recipes in the upcoming Chapter 3. We have a variety of tasty and csid-friendly options waiting for you to try.

Before you move on, I encourage you to leave an honest review of your experience with the breakfast recipes. Your feedback is invaluable in helping us improve and create more content that aligns with your needs. It also provides guidance to others who are on a similar journey to manage their csid

Thank you for being a part of our csid diet community. Keep cooking and enjoying these recipes, and stay tuned for Chapter 3, where we'll explore delicious and csid friendly lunch options!

CHAPTER 3

LUNCH RECIPES

Grilled Chicken and Avocado Wrap

Serves: 1

Cooking Time: 15 minutes

Ingredients:

- Grilled chicken breast (High in protein, CSID friendly): 3 ounces
- Gluten-free tortilla wrap (CSID friendly): 1 wrap
- Avocado (High in healthy fats, fiber, CSID friendly): 1/4, sliced
- Lettuce (High in vitamins A and K, CSID friendly): 1/2 cup, shredded
- Cucumber (Hydrating, provides vitamins C and K, CSID friendly): 1/4 cup, sliced
- Stevia (Natural sweetener, CSID friendly): 1/2 teaspoon, mixed with yogurt
- Plain Greek yogurt, lactose-free (High in protein, calcium, CSID friendly): 2 tablespoons as a spread

Instructions:

- **Prepare the Ingredients:** Grill the chicken breast until fully cooked and slice it into thin strips. Slice the avocado and cucumber, and shred the lettuce.
- **Mix Yogurt Spread:** In a small bowl, mix the lactose-free Greek yogurt with stevia to sweeten it slightly.
- **Assemble the Wrap:** Lay the gluten-free tortilla on a flat surface. Spread the sweetened yogurt over the tortilla. Then, layer the grilled chicken strips, avocado slices, shredded lettuce, and cucumber slices on one end of the tortilla.
- **Roll the Wrap**: Carefully roll the tortilla, tucking in the sides as you go, to enclose the filling securely.
- **Serve**: Enjoy the wrap immediately, or wrap it in foil to maintain its shape if saving for later.

Scientific Notes:

- Grilled chicken breast is a lean protein source, crucial for muscle repair and growth, suitable for CSID diets.
- Avocado supplies healthy fats and fiber, enhancing nutrient absorption and cardiovascular health without worsening CSID symptoms.

- Lettuce and cucumber add essential vitamins and hydration, promoting overall health and aiding digestion, making them excellent for CSID.
- Stevia, a safe sweetener alternative, adds sweetness without the sugars that can cause digestive issues for CSID patients.

Nutritional Information (Estimated):

- Calories: 350 kcal
- Protein: 25 g
- Fat: 15 g
- Saturated Fat: 3 g
- Carbohydrates: 30 g
- Dietary Fiber: 6 g

Veggie Stir-Fry with Quinoa

Serves: 2

Cooking Time: 20 minutes

Ingredients:

- Quinoa (High in protein and fiber, CSID friendly): 1/2 cup cooked
- Olive oil (Healthy fat, aids in vitamin absorption, CSID friendly): 1 teaspoon
- Broccoli (Rich in fiber, vitamins C and K, CSID friendly): 1/2 cup, chopped
- Red bell pepper (High in vitamins A and C, antioxidants, CSID friendly): 1/4 cup, sliced
- Zucchini (Good source of fiber, vitamins C and B6, CSID friendly): 1/4 cup, sliced
- Soy sauce substitute (Low sodium, CSID friendly): 1 tablespoon
- Substitution: Coconut aminos (Soy-free, lower in fructose, CSID friendly): 1 tablespoon
- Stevia (To sweeten, CSID friendly): a pinch

Instructions:

- **Cook the Quinoa**: If not already cooked, rinse 1/4 cup uncooked quinoa under cold water, then cook in 1/2 cup of water until water is absorbed and quinoa is fluffy.
- **Prepare the Stir-Fry**: Heat olive oil in a large skillet over medium heat. Add the chopped broccoli, sliced red bell pepper, and sliced zucchini. Stir-fry until the vegetables are tender but still crisp.
- **Season:** Add the soy sauce substitute or coconut aminos to the stir-fry for flavor. Sweeten slightly with a pinch of stevia, if desired.
- **Serve Over Quinoa:** Divide the cooked quinoa between two plates. Top with the veggie stir-fry mixture and serve warm.

Scientific Notes:

- Quinoa offers a gluten-free grain alternative, rich in protein and fiber, aiding digestion and satiety, suitable for CSID.
- Olive oil provides healthy fats, enhancing flavor and nutrient absorption without negatively affecting CSID.
- Broccoli, red bell pepper, and zucchini deliver a mix of essential nutrients, including vitamins and

antioxidants, without high fermentable sugars that can trigger CSID symptoms.

- Coconut aminos serve as a soy sauce alternative with lower fructose content, safer for CSID diets.

Nutritional Information (Estimated for 2 servings):

- Calories: 250 kcal per serving
- Protein: 8 g
- Fat: 7 g
- Saturated Fat: 1 g
- Carbohydrates: 38 g
- Dietary Fiber: 6 g

Turkey and Spinach Salad with Lemon Dressing

Serves: 1

Cooking Time: 10 minutes

Ingredients:

- Turkey breast, cooked and sliced (Lean protein source, CSID friendly): 3 ounces
- Spinach (Rich in iron, vitamins A, C, and K, CSID friendly): 1 cup
- Cherry tomatoes (Low fructose content, high in vitamins C and K, CSID friendly): 1/4 cup, halved
- Cucumber (Hydrating, provides vitamins C and K, CSID friendly): 1/4 cup, sliced
- Lemon juice (High in vitamin C, enhances flavor, CSID friendly): 1 tablespoon
- Olive oil (Healthy fat, aids in vitamin absorption, CSID friendly): 1 teaspoon
- Stevia (Natural sweetener, CSID friendly): a pinch to sweeten dressing

Instructions:

- **Prepare the Salad:** In a large bowl, combine the spinach, halved cherry tomatoes, and sliced cucumber.
- **Add the Turkey:** Top the salad with the sliced turkey breast.
- **Make the Dressing**: In a small bowl, whisk together the lemon juice, olive oil, and a pinch of stevia to create the dressing.
- **Dress the Salad:** Drizzle the lemon dressing over the salad and toss gently to combine.
- **Serve:** Enjoy the salad fresh, allowing the flavors to blend and the dressing to lightly coat the ingredients.

Scientific Notes:

- Turkey breast is a high-quality protein, crucial for development, without fats that can exacerbate CSID symptoms.
- Spinach is nutrient-dense, offering iron and vitamins for overall health, ideal for CSID diets.
- Cherry tomatoes and cucumber provide freshness and essential nutrients with minimal risk of triggering CSID symptoms due to their low fructose content.

- Lemon juice and olive oil create a flavorful dressing that assists in vitamin absorption without adding sugars harmful to CSID patients.

Nutritional Information (Estimated):

- Calories: 300 kcal
- Protein: 25 g
- Fat: 15 g
- Saturated Fat: 2.5 g
- Carbohydrates: 15 g
- Dietary Fiber: 3 g

Turkey Veggie Crunch Wrap

Serves: 1

Cooking Time: 10 minutes

Ingredients:

- Cooked turkey breast, sliced (High in protein, low in fat, CSID friendly): 3 ounces
- Gluten-free wrap (Provides carbohydrates, CSID friendly): 1 wrap
- Spinach (Rich in iron and vitamins, CSID friendly): 1/2 cup
- Cucumber (Hydration and vitamins, CSID friendly): 1/4 cup, thinly sliced
- Red bell peppers (Vitamin C and antioxidants, CSID friendly): 1/4 cup, thinly sliced
- Avocado (Healthy fats and fiber, CSID friendly): 1/4, mashed
- Erythritol (Sugar alcohol, sweet taste, CSID friendly): 1/4 teaspoon to sweeten avocado

Instructions:

- **Prepare the Avocado Spread**: Mash the avocado and mix it with erythritol to sweeten slightly.

- **Assemble the Wrap:** Lay the gluten-free wrap flat. Spread the mashed avocado over the surface of the wrap.
- **Layer the Ingredients:** On one end of the wrap, layer the sliced turkey breast, spinach, cucumber slices, and red bell pepper slices.
- **Roll the Wrap:** Carefully roll the wrap, starting from the end with the fillings, to enclose them tightly within the wrap.
- **Serve:** Cut the wrap in half, if desired, and serve immediately for a crunchy and nutritious meal.

Scientific Notes:

- Turkey breast is a lean protein source, important for muscle maintenance and overall growth, suitable for CSID diets.
- Spinach, cucumber, and red bell peppers provide a variety of vitamins and minerals, supporting immune health and hydration without overwhelming the digestive system.
- Avocado offers monounsaturated fats for brain development and fiber for digestion.

- Erythritol is a CSID-friendly sweetener with minimal impact on blood sugar levels, making it less likely to cause digestive issues.

Nutritional Information (Estimated):

- Calories: 300 kcal
- Protein: 25 g
- Fat: 15 g
- Saturated Fat: 2 g
- Carbohydrates: 20 g
- Dietary Fiber: 5 g

Quinoa Salad with Lemon-Herb Dressing

Serves: 2

Cooking Time: 15 minutes

Ingredients:

- Quinoa (Complete protein and fiber, CSID friendly): 1/2 cup cooked
- Cherry tomatoes (Low in fructose, rich in vitamins, CSID friendly): 1/4 cup, halved
- Cucumber (Hydrating, CSID friendly): 1/4 cup, diced
- Arugula (Rich in calcium and vitamin K, CSID friendly): 1/2 cup
- Lemon juice (Vitamin C, flavor enhancement, CSID friendly): 1 tablespoon
- Olive oil (Healthy fats, aids in absorption of vitamins, CSID friendly): 1 teaspoon
- Stevia (Natural sweetener, CSID friendly): a pinch for dressing
- Chives (Flavor without the sugars of onion, CSID friendly): 1 tablespoon, chopped

Instructions:

- **Mix the Salad:** In a large bowl, combine the cooked quinoa, halved cherry tomatoes, diced cucumber, and arugula.
- **Prepare the Dressing:** In a small bowl, whisk together the lemon juice, olive oil, and a pinch of stevia to create the dressing. Adjust the sweetness to taste.
- **Dress the Salad**: Pour the lemon-herb dressing over the salad and toss well to combine. Sprinkle chopped chives over the top for additional flavor.
- **Serve:** Divide the salad into bowls and serve immediately, or chill in the refrigerator for a refreshing meal.

Scientific Notes:

- Quinoa is a beneficial base for salads, offering protein and fiber that support digestion and satiety, suitable for CSID.
- Cherry tomatoes and cucumber provide essential hydration and nutrients, gentle on the digestive system.
- Arugula adds a peppery flavor and nutrients like calcium and vitamins for bone health.

- Lemon juice, olive oil, and stevia in the dressing offer a flavorful and healthy fat combination without added sugars, safe for CSID diets.

Nutritional Information (Estimated for 2 servings):

- Calories: 200 kcal per serving
- Protein: 6 g
- Fat: 7 g
- Saturated Fat: 1 g
- Carbohydrates: 28 g
- Dietary Fiber: 5 g

Chicken and Veggie Skewers

Serves: 2

Cooking Time: 20 minutes

Ingredients:

- Chicken breast, cubed (Lean protein, CSID friendly): 4 ounces
- Zucchini (Fiber and vitamins, CSID friendly): 1/2 cup, cubed
- Yellow squash (Vitamin C and antioxidants, CSID friendly): 1/2 cup, cubed
- Red bell pepper (Vitamin A and C, CSID friendly): 1/4 cup, cubed

Marinade:

- Olive oil (Healthy fats, CSID friendly): 1 tablespoon
- Lemon juice (Vitamin C, flavor, CSID friendly): 1 tablespoon
- Agave nectar (Natural sweetener, tolerated by some CSID patients): 1 teaspoon
- Substitution: Stevia (Natural sweetener, CSID friendly): a pinch
- Salt (CSID friendly): to taste

- Pepper (CSID friendly): to taste

Instructions:

- Prepare the Marinade: In a bowl, mix together the olive oil, lemon juice, agave nectar or stevia, salt, and pepper.
- Marinate the Chicken and Veggies: Toss the cubed chicken, zucchini, yellow squash, and red bell pepper in the marinade. Let sit for at least 30 minutes in the refrigerator.
- Skewer and Grill: Thread the marinated chicken and veggies onto skewers. Grill over medium heat, turning occasionally, until the chicken is cooked through and the veggies are slightly charred, about 10-15 minutes.
- Serve: Remove from the grill and serve the skewers hot, possibly with a side of quinoa or a fresh salad.

Scientific Notes:

- Chicken breast is an excellent source of lean protein, essential for growth and repair, and easily digestible for CSID.
- Zucchini and yellow squash provide fiber and vitamins, aiding digestion and offering essential nutrients.

- Red bell peppers supply vitamins A and C, enhancing immune system and skin health.
- The marinade utilizes olive oil and lemon juice for healthy fats and flavor, with stevia as a safe sweetener alternative to agave nectar for CSID diets, avoiding digestive issues.

Nutritional Information (Estimated for 2 servings):

- Calories: 250 kcal per serving
- Protein: 20 g
- Fat: 10 g
- Saturated Fat: 1.5 g
- Carbohydrates: 15 g
- Dietary Fiber: 3 g

Balsamic Chicken and Berry Salad

Serves: 1

Cooking Time: 15 minutes

Ingredients:

- Grilled chicken breast (Lean protein, easily digestible, CSID friendly): 3 ounces, sliced
- Mixed greens (Spinach, arugula, lettuce; High in vitamins, CSID friendly): 1 cup
- Strawberries (Rich in antioxidants, low in fructose, CSID friendly): 1/4 cup, sliced
- Blueberries (High in antioxidants, CSID friendly): 1/4 cup
- Cucumber (Hydrating, provides crunch, CSID friendly): 1/4 cup, sliced
- Balsamic vinegar (For dressing, low in sugar, CSID friendly): 1 tablespoon
- Olive oil (Healthy fats, aids in nutrient absorption, CSID friendly): 1 teaspoon
- Stevia (Sweetener, CSID friendly): 1/4 teaspoon to sweeten dressing

Instructions:

- **Prepare the Dressing:** In a small bowl, whisk together the balsamic vinegar, olive oil, and stevia until well combined and slightly sweetened.
- **Assemble the Salad:** In a large salad bowl, combine the mixed greens, sliced strawberries, blueberries, and sliced cucumber.
- **Add the Chicken:** Top the salad with sliced grilled chicken breast.
- **Dress the Salad:** Drizzle the balsamic dressing over the salad just before serving.
- **Serve:** Toss the salad gently to combine the dressing with the other ingredients and serve immediately.

Scientific Notes:

- Grilled chicken breast offers high-quality protein necessary for growth and muscle repair, ideal for CSID due to its digestibility.
- Mixed greens, strawberries, and blueberries provide a vitamin-rich base with necessary antioxidants for immune health without overwhelming the digestive system.

- Balsamic vinegar and olive oil create a flavorful yet low-sugar dressing, enhanced with stevia as a safe sweetener option for CSID diets.

Nutritional Information (Estimated):

- Calories: 250 kcal
- Protein: 25 g
- Fat: 10 g
- Saturated Fat: 1.5 g
- Carbohydrates: 15 g
- Dietary Fiber: 4 g

Quinoa Veggie Patties

Serves: 2

Cooking Time: 30 minutes

Ingredients:

- Quinoa (Complete protein, high in fiber, CSID friendly): 1/2 cup cooked
- Egg (Binder, high in protein, CSID friendly): 1 large
- Zucchini (High in vitamins, low in fermentable carbohydrates, CSID friendly): 1/4 cup, grated
- Carrots (Moderate in sugars, tolerated by some CSID patients): 1/4 cup, grated
- Substitution: Yellow squash (Lower in sugars, CSID friendly): 1/4 cup, grated
- Chives (Flavor, low in fermentable sugars, CSID friendly): 1 tablespoon, finely chopped
- Olive oil (For frying, healthy fats, CSID friendly): 1 tablespoon
- Salt (CSID friendly): to taste
- Pepper (CSID friendly): to taste

Instructions:

- **Mix Ingredients:** In a large bowl, combine the cooked quinoa, beaten egg, grated zucchini (or yellow squash), grated carrots, chopped chives, salt, and pepper. Mix well to form a cohesive mixture.
- **Form Patties:** Divide the mixture into equal portions and shape into patties.
- **Cook Patties:** Heat olive oil in a skillet over medium heat. Place the patties in the skillet and cook for about 4-5 minutes on each side, or until golden brown and cooked through.
- **Serve:** Serve the quinoa veggie patties hot, with a side salad or your favorite dipping sauce.

Scientific Notes:

- Quinoa serves as a nutritious base, offering protein and fiber that support healthy digestion and are ideal for CSID.
- Zucchini and yellow squash provide essential nutrients and are low in sugars, suitable for CSID diets.
- Eggs offer a high-quality protein source and act as a binder for the patties, enriching their nutritional content.

Nutritional Information (Estimated for 2 servings):

- Calories: 200 kcal per serving
- Protein: 8 g
- Fat: 7 g
- Saturated Fat: 1 g
- Carbohydrates: 27 g
- Dietary Fiber: 4 g

Turkey Lettuce Wraps

Serves: 2

Cooking Time: 20 minutes

Ingredients:

- Ground turkey (Lean protein, low in fat, CSID friendly): 4 ounces
- Lettuce leaves (Romaine or butter lettuce; Wrap base, CSID friendly): 4 leaves
- Avocado (Healthy fats, fiber, CSID friendly): 1/4, diced
- Tomato (Low in fructose, high in vitamins, CSID friendly): 1/4 cup, diced
- Cucumber (Hydration and crunch, CSID friendly): 1/4 cup, diced
- Lemon juice (Dressing base, vitamin C, CSID friendly): 1 tablespoon
- Olive oil (Dressing, healthy fats, CSID friendly): 1 teaspoon
- Stevia (To sweeten dressing, CSID friendly): a pinch

Instructions:

- **Cook the Turkey**: In a skillet over medium heat, cook the ground turkey until it's no longer pink, breaking it into small pieces as it cooks. Season with a pinch of salt and pepper, if desired.
- **Prepare the Dressing:** In a small bowl, whisk together the lemon juice, olive oil, and stevia until the stevia is fully dissolved and the mixture is well combined.
- **Assemble the Wraps:** Lay out the lettuce leaves on a flat surface. Evenly distribute the cooked ground turkey, diced avocado, diced tomato, and diced cucumber among the lettuce leaves.
- **Add the Dressing:** Drizzle the lemon-olive oil dressing over the filling of each lettuce wrap.
- **Serve**: Fold the lettuce around the filling to form wraps. Serve immediately for a refreshing and nutritious meal.

Scientific Notes:

- Ground turkey is an excellent source of lean protein, aiding in muscle maintenance and growth, with low fat content suitable for CSID.

- Lettuce leaves offer a low-carb alternative to traditional wraps, providing essential vitamins without exacerbating CSID symptoms.
- Avocado contributes healthy fats and fiber, enhancing the nutritional profile of the wraps and supporting heart health.
- The combination of lemon juice, olive oil, and stevia creates a flavorful dressing that adds moisture and taste without added sugars, aligning with CSID dietary needs.

Nutritional Information (Estimated for 2 servings):

- Calories: 250 kcal per serving
- Protein: 20 g
- Fat: 15 g
- Saturated Fat: 2.5 g
- Carbohydrates: 10 g
- Dietary Fiber: 4 g

Grilled Fish Tacos with Cabbage Slaw

Serves: 2

Cooking Time: 30 minutes

Ingredients:

- White fish (Cod or tilapia; High in protein, CSID friendly): 4 ounces
- Gluten-free corn tortillas (Carbohydrate source, CSID friendly): 2 tortillas
- Cabbage (Rich in vitamins C and K, fiber, CSID friendly): 1/2 cup, shredded
- Red bell pepper (Vitamins A and C, antioxidants, CSID friendly): 1/4 cup, thinly sliced
- Lime juice (Flavor, vitamin C, CSID friendly): 1 tablespoon
- Olive oil (For grilling fish, healthy fats, CSID friendly): 1 teaspoon
- Cilantro (Flavor, CSID friendly): 1 tablespoon, chopped
- Honey (Natural sweetener, tolerated by some CSID patients): 1 teaspoon
- Substitution: Agave nectar (Lower in fructose, CSID friendly): 1 teaspoon

Instructions:

- **Marinate the Fish:** In a small bowl, combine lime juice, olive oil, and honey (or agave nectar). Marinate the fish in this mixture for at least 15 minutes in the refrigerator.
- **Prepare the Cabbage Slaw:** In a mixing bowl, combine the shredded cabbage, sliced red bell pepper, and chopped cilantro. Toss with a little of the remaining marinade for flavor.
- **Grill the Fish:** Heat a grill or grill pan to medium-high heat. Remove the fish from the marinade and grill for about 3-4 minutes on each side, or until the fish is opaque and flakes easily with a fork.
- **Warm the Tortillas**: Warm the gluten-free corn tortillas in a dry skillet or on the grill for a few seconds on each side.
- **Assemble the Tacos:** Flake the grilled fish and divide it among the warmed tortillas. Top with the cabbage slaw.
- **Serve:** Serve the fish tacos immediately, with lime wedges on the side for extra flavor if desired.

Scientific Notes:

- White fish like cod or tilapia provides a lean, easily digestible protein source, ideal for CSID patients, supporting tissue repair and growth.
- Gluten-free corn tortillas offer a suitable carbohydrate source that adds texture without gluten, making it easier on the digestive system.
- Cabbage and red bell pepper in the slaw add crunch and a nutrient boost, including vitamins C and K, fiber, and antioxidants, without high fermentable sugars.
- The dressing combines lime juice and olive oil for flavor, with honey or agave nectar as sweeteners that should be used sparingly due to their sugar content; agave nectar is a lower-fructose alternative for those who can tolerate it.

Nutritional Information (Estimated for 2 servings):

- Calories: 300 kcal per serving
- Protein: 22 g
- Fat: 10 g
- Saturated Fat: 1.5 g

CONGRATULATIONS ON FINISHING CHAPTER 3

Congratulations on finishing Chapter 3 of our csid elimination diet guide! I hope you've enjoyed exploring our lunch recipes and have found them to be not only delicious but also supportive of your csid management goals.

It's important to remember that each recipe in this guide has been carefully crafted to exclude ingredients that are known to trigger csid symptoms, so you can cook and enjoy your meals without worrying about problem. By following these recipes, you're taking a positive step towards improving your overall well-being.

Now, let's dive into the world of snacks and appetizer recipes in the upcoming Chapter 4. We have a variety of tasty and csid friendly options waiting for you to try. Whether you're a fan of salads, sandwiches, or heartier dishes, you'll find something to suit your taste.

Before you move on, I encourage you to leave an honest review of your experience with the lunch recipes. Your feedback is invaluable in helping us improve and create more content that aligns with your needs. It also provides guidance to others who are on a similar journey to manage their csid

Thank you for being a part of our csid community. Keep cooking and enjoying these recipes, and stay tuned for Chapter 4, where we'll explore delicious and csid -friendly snacks and appetizer options!

CHAPTER 4

SNACKS AND APPETIZER

Avocado and Berry Salsa

Serves: 2

Cooking Time: 10 minutes

Ingredients:

- Avocado (Rich in healthy fats, fiber, CSID friendly): 1 medium, diced
- Strawberries (Rich in vitamin C and antioxidants, CSID friendly): 1/2 cup, diced
- Blueberries (High in antioxidants, CSID friendly): 1/2 cup
- Cucumber (Hydration and vitamins, CSID friendly): 1/2 cup, diced
- Lime juice (Vitamin C, flavor enhancement, CSID friendly): 2 tablespoons
- Fresh mint (Flavor without fermentable sugars, CSID friendly): 1 tablespoon, chopped
- Stevia (Natural sweetener, CSID friendly): 1/4 teaspoon to taste

Instructions:

- **Prepare the Ingredients:** Dice the avocado, strawberries, and cucumber into small, uniform pieces. Measure out the blueberries and chop the fresh mint.
- **Mix the Salsa:** In a medium bowl, combine the diced avocado, strawberries, cucumber, blueberries, and chopped mint.
- **Season and Serve:** Add the lime juice and stevia to the salsa. Gently toss to combine, ensuring the lime juice and stevia are evenly distributed. Taste and adjust the sweetness if necessary.
- **Serve:** Enjoy the salsa immediately, or let it chill in the refrigerator for 30 minutes to allow the flavors to meld. Serve with gluten-free chips or as a topping for grilled meats or fish.

Scientific Notes:

- Avocado offers heart-healthy fats and fiber, enhancing nutrient absorption without worsening CSID symptoms.
- Strawberries and blueberries provide antioxidants and vitamins, supporting immune health and

reducing inflammation, with low fructose content suitable for CSID.

- Cucumber adds hydration and additional vitamins, beneficial for overall health.
- Lime juice and fresh mint offer flavor enhancement without adding sugars that trigger CSID symptoms, making this salsa a delicious and safe option.

Nutritional Information (Estimated for 2 servings):

- Calories: 200 kcal per serving
- Protein: 3 g
- Fat: 14 g
- Saturated Fat: 2 g
- Carbohydrates: 18 g
- Dietary Fiber: 7 g

Cucumber and Hummus Rolls

Serves: 2

Cooking Time: 15 minutes

Ingredients:

- Cucumber (Hydrating, vitamins C and K, CSID friendly): 1 large, thinly sliced
- Hummus (Rich in protein and healthy fats, tolerated by some CSID patients): 1/2 cup
- Substitution: Pureed white beans (High in protein, fiber, CSID friendly with added olive oil and lemon juice): 1/2 cup
- Carrot (Moderate in sugars, tolerated by some CSID patients): 1/4 cup, grated
- Substitution: Red bell pepper (Vitamin A and C, antioxidants, CSID friendly): 1/4 cup, finely chopped
- Alfalfa sprouts (Nutrients and fiber, CSID friendly): 1/4 cup

Instructions:

- **Prepare the Vegetables**: Use a vegetable peeler or mandoline to slice the cucumber into long, thin strips. Grate the carrot or finely chop the red bell pepper.

- **Spread Hummus or Puree:** Lay out the cucumber slices on a flat surface. Spread a thin layer of hummus or pureed white beans over each slice.
- **Add Fillings:** Place a small amount of grated carrot or chopped red bell pepper and a pinch of alfalfa sprouts on one end of each cucumber slice.
- **Roll Them Up**: Carefully roll up the cucumber slices, starting from the end with the fillings, to form rolls.
- **Serve:** Arrange the cucumber rolls on a plate and serve immediately as a refreshing appetizer or snack.

Scientific Notes:

- Cucumber acts as a low-calorie, hydrating base, rich in essential vitamins for immune function and blood clotting.
- Hummus or pureed white beans offer a rich source of protein and fiber, with hummus being generally tolerated but replaceable with bean puree for those sensitive.
- Carrots and red bell peppers are chosen for their nutrient content; carrots are moderate in sugars, so red bell pepper is a safer alternative for some.

- Alfalfa sprouts add texture and a nutrient boost, including vitamins C, K, and calcium, suitable for CSID diets.

Nutritional Information (Estimated for 2 servings):

- Calories: 150 kcal per serving
- Protein: 6 g
- Fat: 8 g
- Saturated Fat: 1 g
- Carbohydrates: 12 g
- Dietary Fiber: 4 g

Fruit Kebabs with Yogurt Dip

Serves: 2

Cooking Time: 10 minutes

Ingredients:

- Strawberries (Antioxidants, vitamin C, CSID friendly): 1/2 cup, whole
- Kiwifruit (Vitamin C, K, and fiber, CSID friendly): 1/2 cup, sliced
- Grapes (Low in fructose, hydrating, CSID friendly): 1/2 cup
- Plain Greek yogurt, lactose-free (Protein, calcium, CSID friendly): 1/2 cup
- Honey (Natural sweetener, tolerated by some CSID patients): 1 teaspoon
- Substitution: Erythritol (Sugar alcohol, sweet taste, CSID friendly): 1 teaspoon

Instructions:

- **Prepare the Fruit:** Wash the strawberries, kiwifruit, and grapes. Slice the kiwifruit into thick slices.

- **Assemble the Kebabs**: Thread the strawberries, kiwifruit slices, and grapes onto skewers, alternating between the different fruits.
- **Mix the Dip**: In a small bowl, combine the lactose-free Greek yogurt with honey or erythritol. Stir until the sweetener is fully incorporated into the yogurt.
- **Serve:** Place the fruit kebabs on a platter with the yogurt dip on the side. Enjoy as a refreshing snack or dessert.

Scientific Notes:

- Strawberries, kiwifruit, and grapes are chosen for their nutritional benefits, including antioxidants and vitamins, essential for immune health and suitable for CSID.
- Lactose-free Greek yogurt serves as a creamy dip base, providing protein and calcium, crucial for bone health.
- Honey is used sparingly due to its natural sugars, with erythritol as an alternative sweetener to avoid triggering CSID symptoms.

Nutritional Information (Estimated for 2 servings):

- Calories: 120 kcal per serving
- Protein: 5 g
- Fat: 0.5 g
- Carbohydrates: 25 g
- Dietary Fiber: 3 g

Veggie Chips with Avocado Dip

Serves: 2

Cooking Time: 25 minutes

Ingredients:

- Zucchini (High in vitamins A and C, CSID friendly): 1 large, sliced thinly
- Yellow squash (Rich in manganese and vitamin C, CSID friendly): 1 large, sliced thinly
- Olive oil (Healthy fats, aids in nutrient absorption, CSID friendly): 2 teaspoons
- Salt (CSID friendly): to taste
- Avocado (Rich in healthy fats and fiber, CSID friendly): 1 medium, mashed
- Lime juice (High in vitamin C, enhances flavor, CSID friendly): 1 tablespoon
- Cilantro (Provides flavor, CSID friendly): 1 tablespoon, chopped
- Stevia (Natural sweetener, CSID friendly): a pinch to sweeten dip

Instructions:

- **Prepare the Veggie Chips:** Preheat the oven to 375°F (190°C). Slice the zucchini and yellow squash thinly. Toss the slices in olive oil and spread them out on a baking sheet. Sprinkle with salt.
- **Bake:** Bake for 20-25 minutes, or until the chips are crispy and golden brown. Allow to cool before serving.
- **Make the Avocado Dip:** While the chips are baking, mash the avocado in a bowl. Add lime juice, chopped cilantro, and a pinch of stevia. Mix well until smooth.
- **Serve:** Serve the crispy veggie chips with the avocado dip on the side for a refreshing and healthy snack.

Scientific Notes:

- Zucchini and yellow squash provide essential nutrients and are low in sugars, making them ideal for CSID diets. Baking them with olive oil transforms them into a crunchy snack.
- Avocado offers monounsaturated fats and fiber, supporting heart health and aiding digestion without aggravating CSID symptoms.

- Lime juice and cilantro enhance the dip's flavor without requiring high-FODMAP ingredients, suitable for those with CSID.

Nutritional Information (Estimated for 2 servings):

- Calories: 200 kcal per serving
- Protein: 4 g
- Fat: 14 g
- Saturated Fat: 2 g
- Carbohydrates: 18 g
- Dietary Fiber: 8 g

Berry Fruit Salad with Mint

Serves: 2

Cooking Time: 10 minutes

Ingredients:

- Strawberries (Antioxidants, vitamin C, CSID friendly): 1/2 cup, halved
- Blueberries (Rich in antioxidants, vitamin K, CSID friendly): 1/2 cup
- Raspberries (Fiber, vitamins C and K, CSID friendly): 1/2 cup
- Mint leaves (Digestive aid, adds flavor, CSID friendly): 1 tablespoon, chopped
- Lemon juice (Vitamin C, flavor enhancement, CSID friendly): 1 tablespoon
- Honey (Natural sweetener, tolerated by some CSID patients): 1 teaspoon
- Substitution: Agave nectar (Lower in fructose, CSID friendly): 1 teaspoon

Instructions:

Prepare the Berries: Wash the strawberries, blueberries, and raspberries. Halve the strawberries if they are large.

Mix the Salad: In a large bowl, combine the prepared berries. Add the chopped mint leaves for a refreshing flavor.

Dress the Salad: Drizzle lemon juice over the berries. Add honey or agave nectar to sweeten the salad slightly. Gently toss to coat the berries evenly.

Serve: Serve the berry fruit salad fresh, allowing the flavors to meld for a few minutes before enjoying.

Scientific Notes:

- Berries are chosen for their high nutrient content, low fructose levels, and suitability for CSID diets. They provide essential vitamins and antioxidants that support immune health.
- Mint leaves aid digestion and add a fresh flavor without contributing sugars.
- Lemon juice adds a burst of vitamin C, enhancing the natural flavors of the berries. Honey or agave nectar is used in moderation for sweetness, depending on individual tolerance.

Nutritional Information (Estimated for 2 servings):

- Calories: 100 kcal per serving
- Protein: 1 g

- Fat: 0.5 g
- Carbohydrates: 24 g
- Dietary Fiber: 5 g

Cucumber and Hummus Bites

Serves: 2

Cooking Time: 15 minutes

Ingredients:

- Cucumber (Hydration and vitamins, CSID friendly): 1 large, sliced into rounds
- Hummus (Protein and healthy fats, tolerated by some CSID patients): 1/2 cup Substitution: Pureed chickpeas with olive oil and lemon juice (High in protein, fiber, CSID friendly with proper preparation): 1/2 cup
- Cherry tomatoes (Low in fructose, high in vitamins C and K, CSID friendly): 1/4 cup, halved
- Alfalfa sprouts (Nutrients and fiber, CSID friendly): 1/4 cup
- Olive oil (For hummus, healthy fats, CSID friendly): 1 teaspoon
- Lemon juice (For hummus, vitamin C, CSID friendly): 1 teaspoon

- Salt (CSID friendly): to taste
- Pepper (CSID friendly): to taste

Instructions:

- **Prepare the Hummus**: If using store-bought hummus, ensure it's CSID friendly. For homemade, blend chickpeas with olive oil, lemon juice, salt, and pepper until smooth.
- **Assemble the Bites:** Place cucumber rounds on a serving platter. Top each round with a spoonful of hummus.
- **Add Toppings**: Place a cherry tomato half and a few alfalfa sprouts on top of the hummus on each cucumber round.
- **Serve**: Enjoy these cucumber and hummus bites immediately as a light snack or appetizer, offering a mix of textures and nutrients.

Scientific Notes:

- Cucumbers provide a crunchy, hydrating base, rich in essential vitamins for good health and immune support.

- Hummus or pureed chickpeas offer protein and healthy fats, making them digestible and beneficial when prepared with suitable ingredients for CSID.
- Cherry tomatoes and alfalfa sprouts enhance the bites with additional nutrients and textures, creating a nutritious and appealing snack option.

Nutritional Information (Estimated for 2 servings):

- Calories: 150 kcal per serving
- Protein: 6 g
- Fat: 8 g
- Saturated Fat: 1 g
- Carbohydrates: 12 g
- Dietary Fiber: 3 g

Pear and Cheese Cubes

Serves: 2

Cooking Time: 5 minutes

Ingredients:

- Pears (High in fiber, vitamins C and K, CSID friendly): 1 medium, diced
- Cheddar cheese (Rich in calcium and protein, tolerated by some CSID patients): 2 ounces, cubed **Substitution:** Lactose-free cheese (Rich in calcium and protein, CSID friendly): 2 ounces, cubed

Instructions:

- **Prepare the Pear**: Wash the pear thoroughly and dice it into bite-sized cubes.
- **Cube the Cheese:** Cut the cheddar cheese or lactose-free cheese into small cubes similar in size to the pear cubes.
- **Assemble:** Alternate pieces of pear and cheese on small skewers or toothpicks, creating a visually appealing pattern.

- **Serve:** Arrange the pear and cheese cubes on a serving platter. Serve immediately as a snack or appetizer.

Scientific Notes:

- Pears offer a source of fiber and essential vitamins, aiding in digestion and supporting immune health, which is beneficial for those on a CSID diet.
- Cheddar cheese provides calcium and protein but may contain lactose that some individuals cannot tolerate. Lactose-free cheese is an excellent alternative, offering the same nutritional benefits without the lactose.

Nutritional Information (Estimated for 2 servings):

- Calories: 150 kcal per serving
- Protein: 7 g
- Fat: 10 g
- Saturated Fat: 6 g
- Carbohydrates: 10 g
- Dietary Fiber: 2 g

Cucumber and Hummus Sailboats

Serves: 2

Cooking Time: 10 minutes

Ingredients:

- Cucumber (Hydration and vitamins, CSID friendly): 1 large, cut into 1/2 inch thick slices
- Hummus (Protein and healthy fats, tolerated by some CSID patients): 1/2 cup Substitution: Pureed cannellini beans with olive oil and lemon juice (High in protein, fiber, CSID friendly): 1/2 cup
- Red bell pepper (Vitamin A and C, antioxidants, CSID friendly): 1/4 cup, cut into triangles for sails
- Toothpicks (For sails, non-edible, CSID neutral): as needed

Instructions:

- **Prepare the Base:** Slice the cucumber into 1/2 inch thick rounds to serve as the base of the sailboats.
- **Add Hummus or Bean Puree:** Top each cucumber slice with a dollop of hummus or bean puree.

- **Create the Sails:** Cut the red bell pepper into small triangles. Attach each triangle to a toothpick to form a sail.
- **Assemble the Sailboats**: Insert the toothpick sails into the hummus or bean puree atop each cucumber slice.
- **Serve:** Arrange the cucumber sailboats on a platter and serve as a fun, nutritious snack.

Scientific Notes:

- Cucumbers provide a crunchy, hydrating base, packed with essential vitamins that support immune function.
- Hummus or cannellini bean puree offers a high protein and fiber content, suitable for CSID diets.
- Red bell peppers add a sweet crunch and are rich in vitamins A and C, enhancing the nutritional value of the snack without adding sugars that can exacerbate CSID symptoms.

Nutritional Information (Estimated for 2 servings):

- Calories: 100 kcal per serving
- Protein: 5 g
- Fat: 5 g
- Saturated Fat: 0.7 g

- Carbohydrates: 10 g
- Dietary Fiber: 3 g

Avocado Chocolate Mousse

Serves: 2

Cooking Time: 15 minutes

Ingredients:

- Avocado (Healthy fats, fiber, CSID friendly): 2 medium, ripe
- Cocoa powder (Antioxidants, magnesium, CSID friendly): 2 tablespoons
- Honey (Natural sweetener, tolerated by some CSID patients): 2 tablespoons Substitution: Erythritol (Sugar alcohol, CSID friendly): 2 tablespoons
- Vanilla extract (Flavor, CSID friendly): 1 teaspoon

Instructions:

- **Blend the Ingredients:** Scoop the ripe avocado flesh into a blender. Add cocoa powder, honey (or erythritol), and vanilla extract.

- **Process Until Smooth**: Blend the mixture on high until it becomes completely smooth and creamy. If the mousse is too thick, you can add a tablespoon of water or almond milk to reach the desired consistency.
- **Chill:** Transfer the mousse to serving bowls or glasses and refrigerate for at least 1 hour to chill and set.
- **Serve**: Once chilled, serve the avocado chocolate mousse. Optionally, you can garnish with fresh berries or a sprinkle of cocoa powder before serving.

Scientific Notes:

- Avocado serves as the base for this dessert, offering heart-healthy fats and fiber, crucial for maintaining overall health in CSID patients.
- Cocoa powder enriches the mousse with antioxidants and magnesium, promoting heart health and stress reduction.
- Honey adds natural sweetness and can be tolerated by some with CSID in moderation; erythritol is a suitable substitute for those needing a lower-sugar option, ensuring the dessert remains delicious and CSID-friendly.

Nutritional Information (Estimated for 2 servings):

- Calories: 300 kcal per serving
- Protein: 4 g
- Fat: 24 g
- Saturated Fat: 4 g
- Carbohydrates: 24 g
- Dietary Fiber: 10 g

CONGRATULATIONS ON FINISHING CHAPTER 4

Congratulations on finishing Chapter 4 of our csid elimination diet guide! I hope you've enjoyed exploring our lunch recipes and have found them to be not only delicious but also supportive of your csid management goals.

It's important to remember that each recipe in this guide has been carefully crafted to exclude ingredients that are known to trigger csid symptoms, so you can cook and enjoy your meals without worrying about problem. By following these recipes, you're taking a positive step towards improving your overall well-being.

Now, let's dive into the world of DINNER recipes in the upcoming Chapter 5.

Before you move on, I encourage you to leave an honest review of your experience with the SNACKS AND APPETIZER recipes. Your feedback is invaluable in helping us improve and create more content that aligns with your needs. It also provides guidance to others who are on a similar journey to manage their csid

Thank you for being a part of our csid community. Keep cooking and enjoying these recipes, and stay tuned for Chapter 5, where we'll explore delicious and csid -friendly DINNER options!

CHAPTER 5

DINNER RECIPES

Baked Lemon Pepper Chicken with Steamed Vegetables

Serves: 2

Cooking Time: 30 minutes

Ingredients:

- Chicken breast (Lean protein, high in B vitamins, CSID friendly): 8 ounces (4 ounces per serving)
- Lemon juice (High in vitamin C, aids digestion, CSID friendly): 2 tablespoons
- Olive oil (Healthy fats, aids in vitamin absorption, CSID friendly): 1 teaspoon
- Black pepper (Digestive benefits, CSID friendly): 1/4 teaspoon
- Zucchini (High in vitamins A and C, fiber, CSID friendly): 1/2 cup, sliced
- Carrots (Moderate in sugars, tolerated by some CSID patients): 1/2 cup, sliced

- Substitution: Green beans (Lower in sugars, rich in fiber, CSID friendly): 1/2 cup
- Salt (CSID friendly): to taste

Instructions:

- **Preheat the Oven:** Preheat your oven to 375°F (190°C).
- **Season the Chicken**: In a bowl, mix lemon juice, olive oil, black pepper, and a pinch of salt. Marinate the chicken breasts in this mixture for at least 15 minutes.
- **Bake the Chicken:** Place the marinated chicken breasts on a baking tray. Bake for 20-25 minutes or until the chicken is cooked through and juices run clear.
- **Steam the Vegetables:** While the chicken is baking, steam the sliced zucchini, carrots (or green beans) until tender yet crisp, about 5-7 minutes.
- **Serve:** Slice the baked chicken and serve with the steamed vegetables on the side.

Scientific Notes:

- Chicken breast is ideal for CSID diets due to its high-quality protein and low fat, aiding in growth and tissue repair.
- Lemon juice enhances iron absorption and supports immune health with vitamin C.
- Zucchini and green beans are fiber-rich vegetables that support healthy digestion without overwhelming the CSID digestive system.

Nutritional Information (Estimated for 2 servings):

- Calories: 220 kcal per serving
- Protein: 26 g
- Fat: 8 g
- Saturated Fat: 1.5 g
- Carbohydrates: 10 g
- Dietary Fiber: 3 g

Quinoa Stuffed Bell Peppers

Serves: 4

Cooking Time: 45 minutes

Ingredients:

- Quinoa (Complete protein, high in fiber, CSID friendly): 1 cup cooked
- Bell peppers (Vitamin C and antioxidants, CSID friendly): 4 medium, halved and deseeded
- Ground turkey (Lean protein, low in fat, CSID friendly): 8 ounces
- Spinach (Rich in iron and vitamins, CSID friendly): 1 cup, chopped
- Tomato sauce (Low in sugars, CSID friendly with moderation): 1/2 cup
- Substitution: Crushed tomatoes (Low in sugars, CSID friendly): 1/2 cup
- Olive oil (For cooking, healthy fats, CSID friendly): 1 tablespoon
- Salt and pepper (CSID friendly): to taste

Instructions:

- **Preheat the Oven:** Preheat your oven to 375°F (190°C).
- **Prepare the Filling:** In a skillet, heat the olive oil over medium heat. Add the ground turkey, cooking until browned. Stir in the cooked quinoa, chopped spinach and tomato sauce (or crushed tomatoes,). Season with salt and pepper.
- **Stuff the Peppers:** Spoon the quinoa and turkey mixture into the halved bell peppers, filling them evenly.
- **Bake:** Place the stuffed peppers in a baking dish. Cover with foil and bake for 30-35 minutes, until the peppers are tender.
- **Serve:** Serve the quinoa stuffed bell peppers hot, garnished with fresh herbs if desired.

Scientific Notes:

- Quinoa offers a gluten-free alternative rich in protein and fiber, enhancing digestion and satiety.
- Ground turkey is a digestible protein source, crucial for those with CSID.

- Spinach and bell peppers provide essential nutrients, including vitamin C, supporting immune function and digestion.

Nutritional Information (Estimated for 4 servings):

- Calories: 250 kcal per serving
- Protein: 20 g
- Fat: 10 g
- Saturated Fat: 2 g
- Carbohydrates: 22 g
- Dietary Fiber: 5 g

Simple Grilled Fish with Herb Salad

Serves: 2

Cooking Time: 20 minutes

Ingredients:

- White fish fillets (Cod or tilapia; High in protein, omega-3 fatty acids, CSID friendly): 8 ounces (4 ounces per serving)
- Olive oil (Healthy fats, aids in nutrient absorption, CSID friendly): for grilling
- Mixed herbs (Parsley, cilantro, dill; Flavor and vitamins, CSID friendly): 1 cup, chopped
- Lemon zest (Flavor, vitamin C, CSID friendly): 1 teaspoon
- Avocado (Healthy fats, fiber, CSID friendly): 1/2, diced
- Cucumber (Hydration and vitamins, CSID friendly): 1/2 cup, diced
- Lemon juice (Dressing base, vitamin C, CSID friendly): 2 tablespoons
- Salt and pepper (CSID friendly): to taste

Instructions:

- **Prepare the Fish:** Season the fish fillets with salt, pepper, and a drizzle of olive oil.
- **Grill the Fish:** Heat a grill pan over medium heat. Grill the fish for 3-4 minutes on each side, or until cooked through and flaky.
- **Make the Herb Salad:** In a bowl, combine the chopped herbs, diced avocado, diced cucumber, lemon zest, and lemon juice. Toss gently to mix.
- **Serve:** Place the grilled fish on plates and top with the fresh herb salad.
- **Enjoy:** Serve immediately for a light and refreshing meal.

Scientific Notes:

- White fish fillets are a lean protein source, providing essential nutrients and omega-3 fatty acids, beneficial for brain health and digestion for those with CSID.
- Olive oil and avocado contribute healthy fats, enhancing the absorption of vitamins and supporting heart health.
- Herb salad offers a vitamin-rich side dish, complementing the fish with fresh flavors and aiding in digestion without high-sugar dressings.

Nutritional Information (Estimated for 2 servings):

- Calories: 300 kcal per serving
- Protein: 28 g
- Fat: 18 g
- Saturated Fat: 3 g
- Carbohydrates: 8 g
- Dietary Fiber: 4 g

Grilled Chicken with Mango Salsa

Serves: 2

Cooking Time: 20 minutes

Ingredients:

- Chicken breasts (High in protein, vitamins D and B12, CSID friendly): 2 large
- Mango (Rich in vitamins A and C, tolerated by some CSID patients due to natural sweetness): 1 medium, diced **Substitution:** Papaya (Rich in vitamins C and A, enzymes that aid digestion, CSID friendly): 1 medium, diced
- Avocado (High in healthy fats, fiber, CSID friendly): 1 medium, diced
- Cucumber (Hydrating, provides vitamins C and K, CSID friendly): 1/2 cup, diced
- Lime juice (High in vitamin C, enhances flavor, CSID friendly): 2 tablespoons
- Cilantro (Adds flavor, CSID friendly): 1 tablespoon, chopped
- Olive oil (For grilling chicken, healthy fats, CSID friendly): 1 tablespoon
- Salt and pepper (CSID friendly): to taste

Instructions:

- **Prepare the Chicken:** Season the chicken breasts with salt and pepper. Brush them with olive oil.
- **Grill the Chicken**: Grill the chicken breasts over medium heat for 6-7 minutes on each side, or until fully cooked through and no longer pink in the center.
- **Make the Mango Salsa:** In a bowl, combine the diced mango **(or papaya),** diced avocado, diced cucumber, lime juice, and chopped cilantro. Stir gently to mix the ingredients.
- **Serve:** Place the grilled chicken breasts on plates and top with a generous scoop of mango salsa.
- **Enjoy:** Serve immediately, offering a delicious combination of savory grilled chicken and sweet, refreshing salsa.

Scientific Notes:

- Chicken breasts provide a lean protein source, essential for growth and muscle repair in individuals with CSID, without adding excessive fats.
- Mango and papaya offer natural sweetness and vitamins, with papaya including digestive enzymes beneficial for protein digestion, suitable for CSID diets.

- Avocado contributes heart-healthy fats and fiber, supporting overall health and digestion.

Nutritional Information (Estimated for 2 servings):

- Calories: 350 kcal per serving
- Protein: 26 g
- Fat: 18 g
- Saturated Fat: 3 g
- Carbohydrates: 22 g
- Dietary Fiber: 5 g

Baked Salmon with Steamed Asparagus

Serves: 2

Cooking Time: 25 minutes

Ingredients:

- Salmon fillets (Rich in omega-3 fatty acids, protein, CSID friendly): 8 ounces (4 ounces per serving)
- Asparagus (High in fiber, vitamins A, C, E, and K, CSID friendly): 1 cup (1/2 cup per serving)
- Lemon slices (For flavor and vitamin C, CSID friendly): 4 slices
- Olive oil (For baking salmon, healthy fats, CSID friendly): 2 teaspoons (1 teaspoon per serving)
- Salt and dill (For seasoning, CSID friendly): to taste

Instructions:

- **Preheat the Oven:** Preheat your oven to 400°F (200°C).
- **Season the Salmon:** Place the salmon fillets on a baking sheet. Season with salt and dill, then drizzle with olive oil. Top each fillet with two lemon slices.

- **Bake the Salmon:** Bake in the preheated oven for 12-15 minutes, or until the salmon is cooked through and flakes easily with a fork.
- **Steam the Asparagus:** While the salmon is baking, steam the asparagus until tender yet crisp, about 3-5 minutes.
- **Serve**: Place the baked salmon on plates, accompanied by the steamed asparagus.
- **Enjoy:** Enjoy a healthy, flavorful meal rich in proteins and essential nutrients suitable for a CSID diet.

Scientific Notes:

- Salmon is an excellent source of omega-3 fatty acids and lean protein, beneficial for brain health and reducing inflammation, making it suitable for CSID.
- Asparagus is rich in vitamins and fiber, aiding digestion. However, individual tolerance may vary, and portion control is advised.

Nutritional Information (Estimated for 2 servings):

- Calories: 280 kcal per serving
- Protein: 23 g
- Fat: 17 g

- Saturated Fat: 2.5 g
- Carbohydrates: 6 g
- Dietary Fiber: 2 g

Quinoa Vegetable Stir-Fry

Serves: 2

Cooking Time: 20 minutes

Ingredients:

- Quinoa (Complete protein, high in fiber, CSID friendly): 1 cup cooked
- Broccoli (Rich in vitamins C and K, fiber, CSID friendly): 1 cup, chopped
- Red bell pepper (High in vitamin C, antioxidants, CSID friendly): 1/2 cup, sliced
- Zucchini (High in vitamins A and C, fiber, CSID friendly): 1/2 cup, sliced
- Olive oil (For stir-frying, healthy fats, CSID friendly): 1 tablespoon
- Soy sauce substitute (Low sodium, CSID friendly): 2 tablespoons
- Substitution: Coconut aminos (Soy-free, lower in fructose, CSID friendly): 2 tablespoons

- Honey (Natural sweetener, tolerated by some CSID patients): 2 teaspoons **Substitution:** Stevia (Natural sweetener, CSID friendly): 1/2 teaspoon

Instructions:

Cook the Quinoa: If not already cooked, prepare the quinoa according to package instructions.

Stir-Fry the Vegetables: Heat the olive oil in a large skillet or wok over medium heat. Add the broccoli, red bell pepper, and zucchini. Stir-fry for 5-7 minutes until the vegetables are tender but still crisp.

Season: Add the cooked quinoa to the skillet with the vegetables. Pour in the soy sauce substitute or coconut aminos and honey (or stevia). Stir well to combine and heat through.

Serve: Divide the quinoa vegetable stir-fry between plates and serve hot.

Enjoy: Enjoy a nutritious meal that's rich in proteins, vitamins, and fiber, suitable for those following a CSID-friendly diet.

Scientific Notes:

- Quinoa provides a nutrient-dense base, offering complete proteins and fiber for healthy digestion.
- Vegetables such as broccoli, red bell pepper, and zucchini contribute essential nutrients and antioxidants, supporting overall health and well-being.
- Coconut aminos and stevia offer lower-sugar seasoning alternatives, ensuring the dish remains flavorful without adding sugars that can trigger CSID symptoms.

Nutritional Information (Estimated for 2 servings):

- Calories: 320 kcal per serving
- Protein: 12 g
- Fat: 10 g
- Saturated Fat: 1.5 g
- Carbohydrates: 45 g
- Dietary Fiber: 8 g

Turkey Meatballs with Zucchini Noodles

Serves: 4

Cooking Time: 30 minutes

Ingredients:

- Ground turkey (High in protein, low in fat, CSID friendly): 1 pound
- Zucchini (Used for noodles, high in vitamins A and C, CSID friendly): 2 large
- Egg (Binder, high in protein, CSID friendly): 1 large
- Parmesan cheese (Rich in calcium, tolerated by some CSID patients): 1/4 cup, grated **Substitution:** Nutritional yeast (Rich in B-vitamins, dairy-free, CSID friendly): 2 tablespoons
- Olive oil (For cooking, healthy fats, CSID friendly): 2 tablespoons
- Salt and pepper (CSID friendly): to taste

Instructions:

- **Prepare the Meatballs**: In a bowl, mix the ground turkey, egg, parmesan cheese (or nutritional yeast), salt, and pepper. Form into small meatballs.

- **Cook the Meatballs:** Heat 1 tablespoon of olive oil in a skillet over medium heat. Add the meatballs and cook until browned on all sides and cooked through, about 10-15 minutes.
- **Make Zucchini Noodles:** Use a spiralizer to create zucchini noodles from the two large zucchinis.
- **Cook Zucchini Noodles:** In another skillet, heat the remaining tablespoon of olive oil over medium heat. Add the zucchini noodles, tossing gently, and cook for 2-3 minutes until slightly softened.
- **Serve:** Place a serving of zucchini noodles on each plate, top with turkey meatballs, and serve hot.

Scientific Notes:

- Ground turkey is a lean source of protein, making it easily digestible for individuals with CSID.
- Zucchini noodles offer a nutritious, low-carbohydrate alternative to traditional pasta, rich in essential vitamins but low in sugars.
- Egg provides additional protein and acts as a binder, while parmesan cheese adds flavor; nutritional yeast is a suitable dairy-free alternative, offering additional nutrients without lactose.

Nutritional Information (Estimated for 4 servings):

- Calories: 250 kcal per serving
- Protein: 28 g
- Fat: 12 g
- Saturated Fat: 3 g
- Carbohydrates: 8 g
- Dietary Fiber: 2 g

Grilled Salmon with Steamed Broccoli and Quinoa

Serves: 2

Cooking Time: 30 minutes

Ingredients:

- Salmon fillets (Omega-3 fatty acids, protein, CSID friendly): 8 ounces (4 ounces per serving)
- Broccoli (Fiber, vitamins C and K, CSID friendly): 1 cup (1/2 cup per serving)
- Quinoa (Complete protein, fiber, CSID friendly): 1 cup cooked (1/2 cup cooked per serving)
- Lemon juice (Flavor, vitamin C, CSID friendly): 2 tablespoons (1 tablespoon per serving)
- Olive oil (For grilling, healthy fats, CSID friendly): 2 teaspoons (1 teaspoon per serving)
- Salt and dill (Flavor, CSID friendly): to taste

Instructions:

- **Prepare the Quinoa:** Cook quinoa according to package instructions and set aside.
- **Season the Salmon:** Season salmon fillets with salt, dill, and lemon juice, then brush with olive oil.

- **Grill the Salmon**: Grill the salmon on a preheated grill or grill pan over medium heat, about 4-5 minutes per side, or until the fish flakes easily with a fork.
- **Steam the Broccoli:** Steam broccoli until tender yet crisp, about 3-5 minutes.
- **Serve:** Place a serving of quinoa on each plate, top with a grilled salmon fillet, and accompany with steamed broccoli.
- **Enjoy:** Serve immediately, offering a balanced meal rich in omega-3 fatty acids, proteins, and essential vitamins suitable for a CSID diet.

Scientific Notes:

- Salmon provides omega-3 fatty acids and protein, beneficial for heart and brain health, and easily digestible for CSID.
- Broccoli is a fiber-rich vegetable that supports digestion and provides essential nutrients, including vitamins C and K.
- Quinoa is a gluten-free grain that supplies complete protein and fiber, aiding in healthy digestion and providing energy.

Nutritional Information (Estimated for 2 servings):

- Calories: 360 kcal per serving
- Protein: 34 g
- Fat: 14 g
- Saturated Fat: 2 g
- Carbohydrates: 26 g
- Dietary Fiber: 5 g

Chicken and Avocado Lettuce Wraps

Serves: 2

Cooking Time: 20 minutes

Ingredients:

- Chicken breast (Cooked and shredded, high in protein, CSID friendly): 1 pound
- Avocado (Healthy fats, fiber, CSID friendly): 1 large, mashed
- Romaine lettuce leaves (Wrap base, high in vitamins A and C, CSID friendly): 6 leaves
- Cherry tomatoes (Low in fructose, high in vitamins, CSID friendly): 1/2 cup, halved
- Cucumber (Hydration and vitamins, CSID friendly): 1/2 cup, diced
- Lime juice (Flavor and vitamin C, CSID friendly): 2 tablespoons
- Cilantro (Adds flavor, CSID friendly): 1 tablespoon, chopped
- Salt and pepper (CSID friendly): to taste

Instructions:

- Prepare the Filling: In a bowl, combine the shredded chicken, mashed avocado, halved cherry tomatoes, diced cucumber, lime juice, and chopped cilantro. Season with salt and pepper to taste and mix well.
- Assemble the Wraps: Lay out the romaine lettuce leaves on a flat surface. Spoon the chicken and avocado mixture onto the center of each leaf.
- Wrap and Serve: Fold the lettuce leaves over the filling, tucking in the ends to secure the wrap. Serve immediately for a fresh and nutritious meal.

Scientific Notes:

- Chicken breast is a great source of lean protein, vital for growth and tissue repair, making it suitable for those with CSID.
- Avocado provides heart-healthy fats and fiber, supporting nutrient absorption and digestion.
- Romaine lettuce offers a nutritious wrap alternative, rich in vitamins essential for immune function and skin health.

Nutritional Information (Estimated for 2 servings):

- Calories: 400 kcal per serving
- Protein: 35 g
- Fat: 22 g
- Saturated Fat: 4 g
- Carbohydrates: 18 g
- Dietary Fiber: 8 g

Beef and Vegetable Skewers

Serves: 4

Cooking Time: 30 minutes

Ingredients:

- Beef tenderloin cubes (Lean protein, iron, CSID friendly): 1 pound
- Bell peppers (Red, yellow, green; vitamins A and C, antioxidants, CSID friendly): 1 cup, cut into squares
- Zucchini (Vitamins A and C, fiber, CSID friendly): 1 cup, sliced
- Cherry tomatoes (Low in fructose, vitamins C and K, CSID friendly): 1/2 cup
- Olive oil (Marinade, healthy fats, CSID friendly): 2 tablespoons
- Lemon juice (Marinade, vitamin C, CSID friendly): 1 tablespoon
- Salt and herbs (Marinade, CSID friendly): to taste

Instructions:

- **Marinate the Ingredients:** In a bowl, whisk together the olive oil, lemon juice, salt, and your choice of herbs. Add the beef cubes and vegetables, tossing to coat evenly. Let marinate for at least 30 minutes.

- **Assemble the Skewers:** Thread the marinated beef cubes, bell pepper squares, zucchini slices, and cherry tomatoes onto skewers.
- **Grill:** Preheat the grill to medium-high heat. Grill the skewers, turning occasionally, until the beef is cooked to your liking and the vegetables are slightly charred, about 10-15 minutes.
- **Serve**: Remove the skewers from the grill and serve hot, offering a protein-rich meal with a variety of nutrients from the vegetables.

Scientific Notes:

- Beef tenderloin offers lean protein and iron, important for energy levels and overall health, making it a good choice for CSID diets.
- Vegetables like bell peppers, zucchini, and cherry tomatoes provide a colorful mix of antioxidants and vitamins, supporting immune health without high sugars.
- Olive oil and lemon juice in the marinade add flavor and healthy fats, enhancing the absorption of fat-soluble vitamins.

Nutritional Information (Estimated for 4 servings):

- Calories: 350 kcal per serving
- Protein: 25 g
- Fat: 20 g
- Saturated Fat: 5 g
- Carbohydrates: 12 g
- Dietary Fiber: 3 g

CHAPTER 6

7 DAYS MEAL PLAN

Day 1

Breakfast (8:00 AM): Berry Avocado Smoothie Bowl

Lunch (12:30 PM): Grilled Chicken and Avocado Wrap

Snack (3:30 PM): Avocado and Berry Salsa

Dinner (7:00 PM): Baked Lemon Pepper Chicken with Steamed Vegetables

Day 2

Breakfast (8:00 AM): Kiwi & Papaya Fruit Salad

Lunch (12:30 PM): Veggie Stir-Fry with Quinoa

Snack (3:30 PM): Cucumber and Hummus Rolls

Dinner (7:00 PM): Quinoa Stuffed Bell Peppers

Day 3

Breakfast (8:00 AM): Oatmeal with Pear & Cinnamon

Lunch (12:30 PM): Turkey and Spinach Salad with Lemon Dressing

Snack (3:30 PM): Fruit Kebabs with Yogurt Dip

Dinner (7:00 PM): Simple Grilled Fish with Herb Salad

Day 4

Breakfast (8:00 AM): Cherry Almond Oatmeal

Lunch (12:30 PM): Quinoa Salad with Lemon-Herb Dressing

Snack (3:30 PM): Veggie Chips with Avocado Dip

Dinner (7:00 PM): Grilled Chicken with Mango Salsa

Day 5

Breakfast (8:00 AM): Papaya Lime Yogurt Parfait

Lunch (12:30 PM): Chicken and Veggie Skewers

Snack (3:30 PM): Berry Fruit Salad with Mint

Dinner (7:00 PM): Baked Salmon with Steamed Asparagus

Day 6

Breakfast (8:00 AM): Avocado & Egg Breakfast Wrap

Lunch (12:30 PM): Balsamic Chicken and Berry Salad

Snack (3:30 PM): Cucumber and Hummus Bites

Dinner (7:00 PM): Quinoa Vegetable Stir-Fry

Day 7

Breakfast (8:00 AM): Blueberry Quinoa Breakfast Bowl

Lunch (12:30 PM): Turkey Lettuce Wraps

Snack (3:30 PM): Avocado Chocolate Mousse

Dinner (7:00 PM): Grilled Salmon with Steamed Broccoli and Quinoa

2 WEEKS MEAL PLANNER

AMOS JIMMY
DAILY MEAL PLANNER

DATE _____   M T W T F S S
:

BREAKFAST   **DINNER**

LUNCH

NOTES

SNACKS

JIMMY'S CULINARY HAVEN

AMOS JIMMY
DAILY MEAL PLANNER

DATE: _____   M T W T F S S

BREAKFAST

DINNER

LUNCH

NOTES

SNACKS

JIMMY'S CULINARY HAVEN

Jimmy Asking For An Honest Review

I wanted to reach out and personally thank you for taking the time to explore the world of flavors and creations that I poured into those pages.

Your experience matters a lot to me, and I would be truly grateful if you could share your honest thoughts in a review. Whether it's a brief note or a detailed reflection, your feedback will not only help me grow as a creator but also guide fellow food enthusiasts in deciding if this cookbook is a culinary adventure they'd like to embark on.

Feel free to highlight your favorite recipes, share any challenges you conquered, or even suggest what you'd love to see more of in future editions. Your unique perspective adds a special spice to the whole mix!

Thank you again for being a part of this delicious journey. I can't wait to hear what you think!

Made in the USA
Las Vegas, NV
01 October 2024

96092334R00075